CHAGALL

Chagall

Text and Notes by
ALFRED WERNER
Author and Lecturer

TUDOR PUBLISHING COMPANY
New York

To Judith

All rights reserved

TUDOR PUBLISHING COMPANY

New York, 1967

Library of Congress Catalog Card Number: 67–19835

Printed in Japan

THE MAGIC OF MARC CHAGALL

Marc Chagall has preserved his unique treasure—*la Chagallité* —mainly because he has managed, to this very day, to retain his childlike naïveté and its concomitant uninhibited fantasy. While he sees the world through the half-frightened, half-amused eyes of a precocious child, his hands are definitely not the hands of a child. In a too materialistic and sophisticated world, he was able not only to hoard his childhood memories, but also to conjure them up, brilliantly, at will, and this without the benefit of a Freudian couch. "To a striking degree, perhaps paralleled only by James Joyce in the field of language," one of his biographers has written, "he has heightened the capacity to transport his symbolic imagery, unalloyed by rational contrivance, from the unconscious to his canvas."

"La Chagal-lité"

The artist was born on July 7, 1887, in the Jewish quarter of the White Russian Vitebsk, on the Dvina River, which was to turn up repeatedly in his work. Chagall's parents were simple, frugal, honest people who, though poor, raised a large family (the elder Chagall worked in the warehouse of a herring monger). As was the custom, Marc, when still a child was sent to the *Cheder,* the Jewish school; thereafter, he attended the public school, where all instruction was given in Russian. When he was still a student there, he discovered his inherent talent—by copying an illustration from a magazine!

Vitebsk

To his parents' alarm, he now wanted to become a painter. Against the wishes of his father, who would have liked Marc to be apprenticed to a shopkeeper or, perhaps, a photographer, but with his mother's support, he enrolled in the local art school. But Marc had learned of the Imperial Academy of Art at St. Petersburg and was determined to study there. He did not attend the

Academy, though, but the school run by the Society for the Protection of the Arts, and thereafter a private class, conducted by Leon Bakst, a progressive painter who was alert to the new influences that came in from the West. In the capital of Tsarist Russia, Chagall, as a Jew, had no residence rights and was in danger of imprisonment; to provide himself with shelter and a livelihood as well as protection, he became a servant in a lawyer's household. Another lawyer, named Vinaver, who was also a member of parliament, admired the young, earnest man's highly untraditional creations—see Plate 8—bought two of his paintings, and even enabled him to go to Paris by giving him a monthly allowance. As Chagall was to put it in his autobiography, *My Life*, written about 1922 (but not published until 1931): "My father put me into the world and Vinaver made a painter of me. Without him I would probably have remained a photographer in Vitebsk without any idea of Paris."

Vinaver

Chagall has spent most of his adult life in France—from 1910 to 1914, from 1923 to 1941, and again the years from 1948 to the present. Had it not been for the two world wars, Chagall might never have left France, except for short travels to various lands. Young and still inexperienced, he fell in love with the City of Light and on his first day went straight to the Salon des Indépendants where he acquainted himself with the work of the moderns. Of course, he later went to the Louvre: "Rembrandt captivated me and more than once I stopped before Chardin, Fouquet, Géricault." He was poor and had to live in the beehive-like *La Ruche* where he had a tiny room, similar to the studios occupied by Modigliani, Léger, Soutine and other impecunious young artists who subsequently were to become famous. He was discovered by the poets Blaise Cendrars and Guillaume Apollinaire who dedicated poems to him; he exhibited in the Salon des Indépendants and, in June, 1914, had his first one-man show, in Berlin, sponsored by the avant-garde critic Herwarth Walden, who edited the progressive review *Der Sturm* (The Storm). Like

First sojourn in France

everybody else, Chagall was unaware of the impending world catastrophe and calmly made a trip to his native city. But he had hardly arrived there when the border was closed. World War I had begun.

*W.W. I—
Russia*

The eight years he was to spend in his native land were crowded with personal events. A happy one was his marriage to his childhood sweetheart, Bella Rosenfeld; a less pleasant one, his being called up to arms. This meant leaving Vitebsk for Petrograd (as St. Petersburg was renamed after the outbreak of the conflict with Germany); yet while he wore a uniform, he was able to find a desk job in a government office and to paint in his free time. He exhibited and even found a devoted collector. In February, 1917, the Tsarist regime was replaced by a republic under Kerensky; eight months later, the Bolsheviks under Lenin took over. Though he was not affiliated with the party of revolution, he was appointed Commissar of Fine Arts in his native city. But his esthetics, influenced by the Cubism of Picasso and anticipating what was to become known as Surrealism, did not please the rather pedestrian party officials who angrily asked: "Why is the cow green and why is the horse flying in the sky? What has that to do with Marx and Lenin?"

*Marriage
to Bella*

*The Revo-
lution*

He also quarrelled with the Suprematists, artists who confined themselves to pure geometrical forms, and resented Chagall's use of recognizable objects of nature. He finally resigned as director of the Academy in Vitebsk and, with his wife and infant daughter, Ida, moved to Moscow. There he made decorations for several theaters and began writing his autobiography. He also volunteered to give instruction to war orphans. But he did not like the political climate. Upon learning that the work he had left in Berlin had made him famous there, he decided to leave Soviet Russia for the capital of the German Republic. To quote from his autobiography: "Neither Imperial Russia, nor Soviet Russia needs me. I am a mystery, a stranger to them. . . . perhaps Europe will love me and, with her, my Russia."

9

From Berlin he moved on to Paris, where he arrived in 1923. The next sixteen years were filled with incessant work, but were otherwise "uneventful." The celebrated dealer and publisher, Ambroise Vollard, commissioned Chagall to do etchings for an edition of *Dead Souls,* the novel by the nineteenth-century Russian Nikolai V. Gogol, and for an edition of La Fontaine's *Fables.* To prepare himself for another assignment by Vollard, etchings illustrating the Bible, Chagall made a journey to Palestine. He also traveled to Holland, where he studied the Rembrandts; to Switzerland (to attend the opening of his large retrospective show in Basel); to Spain, where he was attracted by the El Grecos; to Poland, and then to Italy, where he fell in love with pre-Renaissance painting.

Vollard
and book
illus-
trations

In the thirties, Chagall spent much time working on his Bible illustrations. He had completed one hundred and five plates when, in the summer of 1939, Vollard died. (These pictures were finally published by the firm of Tériade in 1956.) At the outbreak of World War II, Chagall and his wife were living in a small town near Marseilles. They remained there even after the defeat of France, for the town was not occupied by the Germans. But Chagall realized that, since he was a Jew and—in the eyes of the Nazis—a "degenerate" artist as well, he was not safe in a Europe threatened by Hitler's armies. Hence, as soon as the chance was offered him and his family to escape to the United States, he took advantage of it. The Chagalls arrived in New York in June, 1941, just as the Nazis were invading the artist's native Russia.

W.W. II—
Escape
to the
United
States

Chagall's sojourn in the New World was punctuated by tragedy —the death in 1944 of Bella, who had posed for many a picture, had translated his autobiography from Russian into French and had seen him rise to international fame. As for Chagall, he did not feel at ease in New York, unfamiliar with the English language as he was, and unappreciated as his work was by a public ill-equipped to fathom his fantastic symbolism, his anti-naturalistic distortions and exaggerations of both form and color, his irrational "perspective," his indifference to the conventions of gravity. But he was not idle. The fruits of his American interlude included sets and costumes for two ballets, *Aleko* and *The Firebird,* and many, many canvases. It was not, however, before his enormous one-man show at the Museum of Modern Art, New York, and at the Art Institute of Chicago, both in 1946, that American art lovers began to have eyes for the unique poetry, the personal dream world presented by this master.

He went back to France in 1947 and was compensated for the lack of enthusiasm shown by some sections of the French public (which, in the period between the two wars, resented him partly because his Expressionist style was so different from the calm and order of classic French art, and partly because he was a Jew and was regarded as alien despite his French citizenship) by the vast exhibition of his works at the Musée National d'Art Moderne in Paris (the first of the numerous exhibitions he was to have in Europe, Israel, and even Japan). After a stay at Orgeval, a little town not far from Paris, in 1950 he moved to Vence, another small town, near Nice, in the south of France. Two years later he married Valentine (Vava) Brodsky. The couple made many journeys—to Greece, Israel, the United States. In 1966 they gave up their home in Vence and settled in St. Paul de Vence, only a short distance away. *Return to France*

Marriage to Vava

The world paid tribute to genius by bestowing on Chagall a number of highly coveted prizes as well as honorary university degrees. But the master, despite his advanced age, refused to retire idly with his laurels. He even branched out by making pottery and sculpture. He made a series of very large paintings on Biblical themes. After his seventieth birthday, he was showered with commissions: to design stained glass windows for the cathedral of Metz, for the synagogue of the Hadassah Medical Center near Jerusalem, for the United Nations Building in New York. His recent accomplishments include painting a new ceiling for the Opéra in Paris, and making decorations for the new *The Jerusalem Windows*

11

parliament building in Jerusalem and Lincoln Center in New York.

It is no easy task trying to sum up an *œuvre* so enormous in quantity, boundless in its ramifications; there is no genre in art in which he has not tried his hand (and, apart from his autobiography, he has also written essays and even poetry). The task, however, is made somewhat simpler by the fact that Chagall's esthetic philosophy has not changed radically in sixty years. Nor did he ever surrender completely to any of the movements that have stirred the art world since he arrived as a young neophyte in Paris. He could not help being influenced by the Cubists, but his poetical quasi-Cubism, with easily recognizable subject matter, was different from the experiments of the more rigid Cubists, who mercilessly whittled down life and content to geometrical patterns.

Surrealism

Chagall has often been called a forerunner of Surrealism. It is true that the magic word *surréel* was coined by Apollinaire, as spellbound he first gazed at Chagall's early paintings. It is also true that André Breton, often called the Pope of Surrealism, said that with Chagall "the metaphor made its triumphant return to modern painting."

Yet while Chagall admitted that his works were "pictorial arrangements" of images that obsessed him, he repeatedly resisted attempts to pin the label "surrealist" upon him. Separating himself from those Surrealists who insisted that their images were the spontaneous outpourings of the subconscious, he warned: "Fantastic or illogical as the construction of my pictures may seem, I would be alarmed to think that I had conceived them through an admixture of automatism." Determined always to remain the architect of his own dreams, he went on to explain: "Even if by automatism one has succeeded in composing some good pictures or in writing some good poems, that does not justify us in setting it up as a method. . . . I am afraid that as a conscious method, automatism engenders automatism."

Style

Chagall remains a creator, consciously building his world out of apparently disparate elements, bringing order out of the chaos of the countless recollections, hopes, fears and frustrations. Nor is he an Expressionist, if one uses that term to denote work like that of the German *Brücke* group and related artists. The category "Expressionism" includes him only insofar as he, like most modern artists, rejects the imitation of the outer world of reality for the expression of an inner world of feeling and imagination, and insofar as his work is characterized by spontaneous, free, intuitive distortion or exaggeration of the ordinary forms and colors of nature in order to achieve an emotional or esthetic effect (to stick to the definition of Expressionism given by a Museum of Modern Art catalogue). Yet his work is more "decorative" than that of the Expressionists, closer to the overall grace and subtle charm of a Gauguin (one of Chagall's favorites) than to the turbulent nightmares of a Munch or a Van Gogh. One is often reminded of Gauguin by Chagall's large curvilinear forms, arrived at through broad, rich, pleasing colors applied in rhythmic, musical roundnesses of a lyrical, poetic quality. Nonnaturalistic colors are, on the whole, favored above local colors. There is little of the academic painters' orthodox perspective, little modeling; there are no shadows, no deep spaces.

The decorative element

Chagall's simplifications often call to mind what a child, or a peasant painter might have done. Now it is correct to say that Chagall, to an amazing degree, has retained the naïveté which endeared him at twenty-three to so many cultivated Parisians. But this naïveté, one way or another, is characteristic of many creative persons who always look at the world with astonished eyes. No child could have designed such a complicated picture as *I and the Village*, or produced the many-faceted Jerusalem windows. Nor could a folk artist have done it (though it goes without saying that in his youth Chagall looked with deep interest at whatever Russian popular art he encountered in or around Vitebsk).

It is to his credit that through all those years, without becoming slick or smug, Chagall was able to preserve his peculiar treasure, *"la Chagallité,"* even in the sophisticated salons of the great cities in which he has moved. In a blasé world he managed to preserve his childhood memories, and to conjure them up at will. He is a special case in modern art, that of the pure and simple in heart, as opposed to the more cerebral geniuses (of which Picasso is a striking example).

To this very day he has remained a child of the ghetto. He practiced his art in Russia for no more than twelve years—as compared to the forty-odd years he painted in the Western world. Yet, although he once fondly called Paris "my second Vitebsk," and has, indeed, been inspired by Parisian vistas and by various landscapes in France, the locale for most of his works is his native city, more precisely, its Jewish section. Aloof though he has been to all isms in art, he has surrendered to Hasidism, that Jewish philosophy that prevailed among the ghetto dwellers, largely untutored, but filled by a metaphysical thirst, that revolt against rigid and shallow rationalism. Hasidism is a philosophy of love, and Chagall is the painter of love. He loves flowers and animals, he loves people, he loves love. There is sadness in his paintings—but rarely the agony of boundless despair. There is always a metaphysical hope deeper than the platitude about the cloud and the silver lining. When he paints a beggar in snow, he puts a fiddle in his hands, and if he sets a mournful rabbi on the canvas, he adds to this symbol of sorrow an innocent white cow, a symbol of the peace of the universe.

The painter of love

ALFRED WERNER

SELECTED BIBLIOGRAPHY

Marc Chagall

(Only books in English and French are listed.)

Chagall, Marc: *Ma Vie*. Paris, 1931. English Translation: *My Life*. New York, 1960.

Schwob, René: *Marc Chagall et l'âme juive*. Paris, 1931.

Sweeney, James Johnson: *Marc Chagall*. New York, 1946.

Maritain, Raissa: *Marc Chagall ou l'orage enchanté*. Geneva, 1948.

Ayrton, Michael: *Chagall*. London, 1950.

Estienne, Charles: *Chagall*. Paris, 1951.

Kloomok, J.: *Marc Chagall, His Life and Work*. New York, 1951.

Venturi, Lionello: *Marc Chagall*. New York, 1956.

Lassaigne, Jacques: *Marc Chagall*. Paris, 1957.

Brion, Marcel: *Marc Chagall*. New York, 1961.

Meyer, Franz: *Marc Chagall*. New York, 1961.

Freund, Miriam: *Jewels for a Crown: The Story of the Chagall Windows*. New York, 1962.

Damase, Jacques: *Chagall*. London, 1963.

Cassou, Jean: *Chagall*. New York, 1965.

Cogniat, Raymond: *Chagall*. New York, 1965.

Erben, Walter: *Marc Chagall*. New York, 1966.

Lassaigne, Jacques: *Marc Chagall: The Ceiling of the Paris Opera*. New York, 1966.

Foster, Joseph K.: *Marc Chagall: Posters & Personality*. New York, 1966.

MARC CHAGALL

1887   Born in Vitebsk, White Russia, on July 7. Eldest child of Zahar and Feiga-Ita Segal.

1906   Studies at the School of Painting, under Yehuda Penn. Apprenticed as a retoucher to a photographer.

1906–07   In the winter, travels to St. Petersburg with a classmate. Fails entrance examination to Baron Stieglitz' School of Applied Art.

1907   Awarded scholarship by art school sponsored by the Imperial Society for the Furtherance of the Arts, St. Petersburg.

1908   Continues art studies at a private school directed by Saidenberg, and under Leon Bakst at the progressive Svanseva School, St. Petersburg.

1909   On one of his visits home, meets Bella Rosenfeld, daughter of well-to-do jeweler.

1910–14   August (1910): a generous patron, the lawyer and Duma deputy, Vinaver, makes it possible for Chagall to go to Paris. Attends two art schools, the Palette (where Le Fauconnier and Segonzac teach) and the Grande Chaumiére. Lives for a while in *La Ruche* (The Beehive), where many young, impecunious artists have their studios. Meets the poets Blaise Cendrars and Guillaume Apollinaire, who write enthusiastically about him. Exhibits three pictures in the *Salon des Indépendants* (1912). Meets the Berlin art dealer, Herwarth Walden, through Apollinaire (1913).

1914   May: Chagall leaves for Berlin, to attend the opening of his one-man show at Walden's *Sturm* Gallery (40 oils and 160 works in other media). In June, he travels to Vitebsk, to attend a sister's wedding and to see Bella again. The outbreak of World War I prevents him from returning to Paris.

1915   Sends 25 pictures to exhibition in the Mikhailova Art Salon in Moscow. Marries Bella (July 25).

1917   October: Bolshevist Revolution. Acquires full rights of citizenship which had been withheld from Jews by the Tsarist regime.

1918   First monograph on Chagall (by A. Efross and J. Tugendhold). Appointed Commissar for Fine Arts in Vitebsk. Organizes celebrations for the anniversary of the October Revolution.

1919   Director of the newly established Free Academy of Art in Vitebsk. Participates in the First State Exhibition of Revolutionary Art in the Petrograd Palace of Art. One room is reserved for his works, which are acquired by the State.

1920–22   May (1920): leaves for Moscow. Designs stage sets for Gogol's *Inspector General* and Synge's *Playboy of the Western World*. Meets Alexander Granowsky, manager of the Chamber State Jewish Theater in Moscow and makes numerous decors for that theater. In 1921 teaches art at two War Orphans Colonies outside Moscow.

1922–23   Summer: Obtains a passport, with the help of Lunacharsky, commissioner of education, and goes to Berlin, where he is subsequently joined by his wife and their young daughter, Ida. Remains in Berlin to autumn, 1923. The dealer Paul Cassirer plans to publish an illustrated edition of Chagall's memoirs, written in Russian, but the project is abandoned. Instead, Cassirer issues Chagall's illustrations in a portfolio, comprising twenty etchings and entitled *My Life*.

1923   September 1: Chagall reaches Paris (his family joins him shortly thereafter). The dealer Ambroise Vollard commissions him to make illustrations for Gogol's *Dead Souls* and La Fontaine's *Fables*.

1924   First retrospective exhibition in Paris (Galerie Barbazanges-Hodebert). Stays at the island Bréhat, off the coast of Brittany.

1926   First one-man show in New York (Reinhardt Galleries).

1927   Does nineteen gouaches, "Cirque Vollard."

1930   Brief visit to Berlin for the opening of the exhibition of the gouaches for the *Fables* (Galerie Flechtheim). Commissioned by Vollard to do etchings for a Bible edition.

1931   Accompanied by wife and daughter, visits Egypt, Lebanon, and Palestine.

1932   Journey to Holland.

1933   Large retrospective exhibition in the Kunsthalle, Basle.

1934   Journey to Spain.

1935   Journey to Poland.

1937   Becomes a French citizen. Journey to Italy. Several of his works included in the Nazi's "Degenerate Art" exhibition in Munich.

1938   Exhibition in Brussels.

1939	Resides in the Loire District.
1940	When France is defeated by the Germans and an armistice is concluded, Chagall and his family are staying at Gordes, a village in Provence, in Unoccupied France.
1941	The Chagalls move to Marseilles. On May 7, they leave Marseilles for the United States, arriving in New York on June 23.
1942	Commissioned by the Metropolitan Opera to do sets for the ballet *Aleko,* based on a story by Pushkin, with music by Tchaikowsky. The work is done in Mexico City, where the first performance is given.
1944	Bella Chagall dies in New York City on September 2.
1945	Sets and costumes for the Metropolitan Opera ballet, *The Firebird,* with music by Stravinsky.
1946	Large one-man show at the Museum of Modern Art, New York, subsequently seen at the Art Institute of Chicago (in the two decades to follow exhibitions throughout the world). Makes journey to Paris.
1947	Revisits Paris for the opening of his exhibition at the Musée National d'Art Moderne.
1948	August: Chagall returns to live in France. Settles at Orgeval, a village near Saint-Germain-en-Laye. At the Venice Biennale, a room for Chagall in the French Pavilion. Awarded the Biennale prize for graphic art.
1949	Sojourn in Southern France. Meets publisher Tériade who is to issue his Bible etchings and other graphic works.

1950	Settles in Vence, near Nice, where he acquires the villa "Les Collines." Show at the Galerie Maeght, in Paris, includes ceramics.
1952	Marriage to Valentine ("Vava") Brodsky. Journey to Greece.
1954	Second journey to Greece.
1955	Makes a ceramic mural, marble reliefs, and other works for the church Notre-Dame-de-Toute-Grâce on the Plateau d'Assy, in the French Alps.
1957	Journey to Israel.
1958	Accepts invitation to give a lecture at the University of Chicago.
1959	The American Academy of Arts and Letters make him an honorary member. Degree of *Doctor honoris causa* conferred by Glasgow University.
1959–60	Designs first of two stained-glass windows for the Cathedral at Metz.
1960	Shares with Oskar Kokoschka the Erasmus Prize, awarded by the European Foundation for Culture in Copenhagen. Degree of *Doctor honoris causa* conferred by Brandeis University, Waltham, Massachusetts.
1961	Designs windows for the synagogue of the Hadassah Medical Center near Jerusalem.
1962	Journeys to Israel for the installation of the windows. Second window for the Cathedral of Metz. Made honorary citizen of Vence.
1963	Journeys to Washington, D.C. to address Congress on behalf of the Center for Human Understanding.

1964   Unveiling of his ceiling for the Paris Opera, commissioned by the minister of culture, André Malraux.

1966   Journey to New York for the unveiling of two murals for the Lincoln Center.

1967   Journey to New York to attend the premiere of a new production of Mozart's *Magic Flute*, for which he had designed the stage sets and costumes.

LIST OF COLOR PLATES

51. Blue Circus. 1950.
52. King David. 1952.
53. Liberation. 1937–52.
54. *Upper:* The Red Rooster. 1952.
    Lower: The Brown Horse. 1952.
55. Good Morning over Paris. 1952.
56. The Artist with a Palette and a Model. 1952.
57. Visions of Paris. 1952.
58. Banks on the Seine. 1953.
59. Red Roofs. 1953.
60. The Flute Player. 1954.
61. Quai de Bercy. 1952.
62. The Bastille. 1954.
63. *Upper Left:* Night in Paris. 1952. *Upper Right:* Eiffel Tower with Donkey. 1954. *Lower Left:* On Sundays. 1954. *Lower Right:* Quai aux Fleurs. 1954.
64. The White Window. 1955.
65. *Upper Right:* Black Water Pitcher. 1955. *Lower Left:* Red Dish. 1955.
66. The Bible. 1956.
67. Moses Breaking the Tablets of the Law. 1955–56.
68. Equestrienne. 1957.
69. Trick Cyclists. 1957.
70. *Upper:* The Red Rooster. 1957. *Lower:* The Accordion Player. 1957.

71. The Lovers of Vence. 1958.
72. Clowns at Night. 1957.
73. Île Saint-Louis. 1959.
74. The Red Circus. 1956–60.
75. The Tree of Jesse. 1960.
76. Woman with Blue Face. 1960.
77. The Bible. 1958–59.
78. The Farmer. 1961.
79. Daphnis and Chloe. 1961. *Upper:* Springtime on the Meadow. *Lower:* Phileta's Orchard.
80. Chloe is Carried off by the Methymneans.
81. Daphnis and Chloe. 1961.
82. *Upper:* Temple and History of Bacchus. *Lower:* Megacles Recognizes his Daughter during the Feast.
83. Moses and the Tablets of the Law. 1962.
84. The Jerusalem Windows. 1960–61. Levi. (Gouache.)
85. Levi. (Lithograph.)
86. Zebulun. (Gouache.)
87. Zebulun. (Lithograph.)
88. Joseph. (Lithograph.)
89. Joseph (detail).
90. Issachar. (Lithograph.)
91. Asher (detail).
92. Self-Portrait. 1962.

NOTES ON THE PLATES

1. Chagall in his studio in Vence. The artist lived in this small town in southern France, not far from Nice, from 1949 to 1966. Visible on the right is the left margin of *Blue Circus* (Plate 51).

2. UPPER: *The Little Parlor*. 1908. Oil. France, Private Collection. This is a room in the house of Chagall's paternal grandfather, a butcher, at Lyozno, a village near Vitebsk. Following the advice of Leon Bakst, his teacher at St. Petersburg, the artist, as a beginner, limited himself to a few colors only. Here, pink and green dominate. This picture was Chagall's first at Bakst's school. LOWER: *Studio*. 1910. Oil. Owned by the artist. This was painted soon after Chagall arrived in Paris and, with its green, red and yellow, shows the influence of the Fauve movement (the "Wild Beasts," led by Matisse). But there are also reminiscences of Van Gogh's *Night Café*.

3. *Still Life with a Lamp*. 1910. Oil. Lucerne, Private Collection. Note the unorthodox perspective, and the arbitrary colors in the two profiles. A strong light radiates from the lamp in the center.

4. *Harvest*. 1910. Oil. New York, Private Collection. Here, too, erupt fervent colors: the yellow of the blouse and the red of the skirt. Mystery is created by the blue branches of the tree.

5. *Homage to Apollinaire*. 1911–12. Oil. Eindhoven, Stedelijk van Abbe-Museum. The dual being—Adam and Eve with the apple—is placed in the center of the disk. In the lower left, the heart, pierced by an arrow, is surrounded by the names of the poet G (for Guillaume) Apollinaire, the German writer (Herwarth) Walden, who ran an art gallery in Berlin, the poet (Blaise) Cendrars, and the writer (Riciotto) Canudo, editor of an avant-garde periodical. All four helped and encouraged young Chagall.

6. *I and the Village*. 1911. Oil. New York, The Museum of Modern Art. In this picture, as in the preceding one, and in some of the paintings to follow immediately, Cubist influence is noticeable. The green-faced youth looks at a white cow, in whose head is a milking scene. Note the upside-down position of the peasant girl and two of the houses.

7. *The Holy Drosky Driver*. 1911. Oil. Krefeld, Private Collection. Behind the serpentine figure is a snow scene, with a church in the background. Chagall composed this picture with the man seated and the church upside-down; Walden however, hung it in his gallery the way it appears here.

8. *Self-Portrait with Seven Fingers*. 1912. Oil. Amsterdam, Stedelijk Museum. The picture received its name from the number of fingers on the subject's left hand. Through the window at the upper left, the Eiffel Tower can be seen, and on the wall beside it, the word "Paris" in Hebrew characters. Also inscribed on the dark-red wall in Hebrew characters is "Russia," referring to the vision of Vitebsk, floating above the clouds at the upper right.

9. *The Poet, or Half-Past Three*. 1911. Oil. Philadelphia, Museum of Art. Just as the *Self-Portrait with Seven Fingers* is a homage to "the Painter," this picture is dedicated to "the Poet" (in the act of writing). Chagall himself wrote many poems. A picture like this may have inspired Apollinaire to coin the term "Surrealism."

10. *Adam and Eve*. 1912. Oil. St. Louis, City Art Museum. This picture shows better than any other the extent Chagall permitted himself to be influenced by the Cubism of Picasso and Braque. Eve (on the right) is seen plucking an apple from the tree and gripping Adam's raised arm.

11. *Still Life*. 1912. Oil. London, Private Collection. Like the Cubists, mentioned above, Chagall here turns to the depiction of objects used in everyday life. Note the glow of the colors.

12. *Pregnant Woman*. 1913. Oil. Amsterdam, Stedelijk Museum. Chagall

seems to have been inspired by the Byzantine Madonnas frequent in old Russian icons. Wearing a dress patterned with flowers, the woman looks like a doll. Her left hand points to the child in her womb. Note the Russian wooden houses, the face above, and the goat in the sky.

13. *The Soldier Drinks.* 1912–13. Oil. New York, The Solomon R. Guggenheim Museum. The soldier, with a curled mustache, is helping himself to a cup of tea from the large samovar. His cap floats over his head. A dancing peasant couple is in the foreground.

14. *Green Violinist.* 1918. Oil. New York, The Solomon R. Guggenheim Museum. The fiddler represents the artist's Uncle Neuch, who "played the violin like a cobbler" (*My Life*).

15. *Burning House.* 1913. Oil. New York, The Solomon R. Guggenheim Museum. This picture refers to a conflagration in the ghetto of Vitebsk: "at the very moment I was born a great fire broke out. . . . The town was on fire, the quarter where the poor Jews lived. They carried the bed and the mattress, the mother and the babe at her feet, to a safe place at the other end of town" (*My Life*).

16. *Self-Portrait in Front of a House.* 1914. Oil. Paris, Private Collection. He painted this picture after returning to his native city. The Russian term for this kind of wooden house is *izba*.

17. *Over Vitebsk.* 1914. Oil. Toronto, Private Collection. Chagall painted several versions of this motif. An old man, with a heavy sack on his back and a stick in his hand, floats above the houses which are surrounded by deep snow. The Ilytch church of Vitebsk is on the right.

18. *Lovers in Blue.* 1914. Oil. Leningrad, Private Collection. This picture, bathed in an eerie blue light, celebrates the artist's reunion with his childhood sweetheart, Bella. She had just returned to Vitebsk after finishing her

studies at a girls' college in Moscow, and had received her rich parents' permission to marry the impecunious artist.

19. *The Mirror*. 1915. Oil. Leningrad, State Russian Museum. In an old-fashioned gilt-framed mirror the oil lamp is reflected. Note the tiny figure of Bella slumbering at the table and making the lamp appear enormous.

20. *Purim*. 1916–18. Oil. Philadelphia Museum of Art. Purim is a joyous festival, celebrated in the twelfth month of the Jewish calendar (corresponding generally to either February or March), reminding the Jewish people of their deliverances from serious dangers in the remote past. Masks like those held by the two figures are customarily worn in the performances staged at this holiday.

21. *Double Portrait with Wineglass*. 1917. Oil. Paris, Musée National d'Art Moderne. Chagall, seated on his wife's shoulders, raises his glass to the joy of living. An angel hovers, in a gesture of benediction, above the cheerful pair. Or is it their baby daughter Ida?

22. *Promenade*. 1917. Oil. Leningrad, State Russian Museum. Weightless, Bella is whirled on her husband's arm high up in the air. A flower-patterned cloth is on the grass, and there is a pink church in the background.

23. *Cemetery Gate*. 1917. Oil. Basel, Private Collection. Inscribed on the gate are verses from the Bible, prophesying that the dead will rise again.

24. *The Lovers and the Lilies*. 1922–25. Oil. New York, Private Collection. Below the strikingly beautiful bouquet of flowers, the young pair embrace in a gesture of tenderness.

25. *Double Portrait*. 1924. Oil. Paris, Private Collection. With the clarity of an old medallion, the painter and his wife are seen in profile.

26. *Ida at the Window.* 1924. Oil. Amsterdam, Stedelijk Museum. The Chagall family spent the summer of 1924 on the island of Bréhat, off the north coast of Brittany. The daughter, Ida, seated on the window sill, is looking out into the landscape. This is one of Chagall's few pictures without symbolic allusions, and among the first free of Cubist features.

27. *Woman with Pigs.* 1926. Gouache. Winnipeg, Private Collection. This is one in the series of illustrations Ambroise Vollard commissioned for an edition of La Fontaine's *Fables.*

28. *Equestrienne.* 1927. Oil. Prague, Narodnie Galerie. Chagall spent many an evening at the Cirque d'Hiver in Paris, as a guest of Vollard, who had a box for the season. The series of gouaches, made at the dealer's request, is now known as Le Cirque Vollard. There are also several small oils on the circus theme.

29. *Flowers.* 1928. Oil. Paris, Private Collection. Chagall did many pictures of flowers in a vase. Often—as is here the case—small figures appear among the flowers or near the bottom of the vase.

30. *Bride and Groom with Eiffel Tower.* 1928. Oil. Paris, Private Collection. Here again is this landmark of Paris, seen already in the early *Self-Portrait with Seven Fingers* (Plate 8). Note the flower angel.

31. *The Girl Acrobat.* 1930. Oil. Paris, Musée National d'Art Moderne. Like Toulouse-Lautrec before him, and like his coeval, Pablo Picasso, Chagall is fond of the world of gay entertainment. In the background is a Romanesque portal.

32. *Equestrienne.* 1931. Oil. Amsterdam, Stedelijk Museum. A man puts his arm around the waist of the circus rider. The horse hugs a violin against its neck.

33. *Bride and Bridegroom.* 1930. Oil. Florida, Private Collection. The

couple are standing on the bank of a river, probably the Dvina, which flows through Vitebsk. Indeed, the background buildings seem more Russian than French.

34. *The Wailing Wall*. 1932. Tel Aviv, Municipal Museum. In 1931 the artist, commissioned by Vollard to make etchings for an edition of the Bible, journeyed to Palestine with his family. The Wailing Wall, in the old city of Jerusalem, is the last remnant of the Second Temple. For many centuries, until it was annexed by the Kingdom of Jordan, it was a place of prayer for orthodox Jews. This is, perhaps, the most realistic picture Chagall has ever painted.

35. *The Lovers at the Eiffel Tower*. 1938–39. Oil. Here, many of the favorite motifs of the artist are combined in a single composition.

36. *Time Is a River without Banks*. 1939. Oil. New York, The Museum of Modern Art. Since it is unusual for Chagall to provide symbolic titles of this kind, this one may have been suggested by an erudite friend from the passages in the *Meditations* of Marcus Aurelius: "Time is a sort of river of passing events, and strong is its current; no sooner is a thing brought to sight than it is swept by and another takes its place, and this too will be swept away."

37. *The Cellist*. 1939. Oil. London, Private Collection. The torso of this double-faced musician is the instrument he is playing, in front of a snow-covered East European town. Note the animal-headed small violinist in the lower right corner.

38. *Obsession*. 1943. Oil. France, Private Collection. Christ on the Cross; a man carrying a huge candelabrum; a woman and child on a cart drawn by a blue horse; a figure floating through the air; a burning house—all of this symbolizes conflagration, destruction and misery (this work was produced in the middle of World War II).

39. *War*. 1943. Oil. Paris, Musée National d'Art Moderne. A horse rears

in the foreground, as if hit by a bullet. A mother, with a child in her arms, seems to escape on a horse-drawn sleigh; a dead man lies on the road, his arms outstretched in the manner of Christ on the Cross; a refugee (in the lower left corner) flees with a bundle on his shoulder; the foreground is filled with ominous red. All this serves to symbolize man's inhumanity to man.

40. *Listening to the Rooster*. 1944. Oil. New York, Private Collection. The cow has two human heads, one male, one female. A fiddler, barely discernible, sits on the cock's rump.

41. *Around Her*. 1945. Oil. Paris, Musée National d'Art Moderne. Chagall's wife died on September 2, 1944. The man with the upside-down head is the painter at his easel, holding a palette. Facing him is Bella, weeping, her head slightly leaning toward a circle that contains a view of Vitebsk. In the upper right corner is a· pair of lovers; the bride wears a long white train. The picture is a testimony of grief, but also of never-ending love.

42. *The Flying Sleigh*. 1945. Oil. New York, Private Collection. A peasant family in a rustic sleigh, drawn high above the wintry landscape by a horse with the head of a cock.

43. *Autumn Village*. 1939–45. Oil. Hartford, Wadsworth Athenaeum. In the tree are two familiar motifs—the fiddler and the white cow. Reclining on the pointed roofs is a bare-breasted woman.

44. *Self-Portrait with Wall Clock*. 1947. Oil. Owned by the artist. We find here again the floating grandfather's clock (see Plate 36) and a figure of Christ on the Cross (see Plate 38).

45. *The Falling Angel*. 1923–47. Oil. Basel, Kunstmuseum. The heavy-breasted angel is falling out of the dark sky. Many motifs, including a Crucifixion, that have appeared in earlier pictures, are here recognizable again. In the lower left, a bearded Jew holds a Torah scroll.

46. *The Dance* (detail). 1950. Oil. Owned by the artist. The artist's interest in the dance is also demonstrated in the decors he made for two ballets, for the ceiling of the Opéra in Paris, and for the Metropolitan Opera, Lincoln Center, New York. Not visible is the left side of the picture, showing a donkey-headed musician and, next to him, a pair of lovers.

47. Color lithograph, one of a series of thirteen illustrations for *Arabian Nights*, commissioned by Pantheon Books, New York. 1941. Chagall gave his fantasy free rein to illustrate the wonderful Eastern stories in the Arabic language that are also known as the *Thousand and One Nights*, told by Sheherazade to her royal husband.

48. Four color lithographs from the same series.

49. *The Fishes at Saint-Jean*. 1949. Gouache. Paris, Private Collection. The green is the narrow peninsula halfway between Nice and Monte Carlo, where Chagall was enchanted by the concert of sea, land and sky.

50. *The Red Sun*. 1949. Oil. Owned by the artist. This painting hung in the entrance hall of Chagall's house at Vence. Note the man reading a book. There is also a tiny bridal couple, upside-down, under a canopy. Barely visible at the lower edge is the artist with easel and palette.

51. *Blue Circus*. 1950. Oil. Owned by the artist. This is the painting whose left margin is visible in Plate 1.

52. *King David*. 1952. Oil. Owned by the artist. One of the numerous large pictures on Biblical themes made by Chagall in the 1950's. (They will be assembled in a building dedicated to Chagall's work by the city of Nice.) Opposite the harp-playing king is Bathsheba (in a long white train), introduced by an angel holding a lighted candelabrum. A boy descends from the sky to bring her flowers. In the lower right corner sits the prophet Nathan, while in the center the red sun sheds its rays on the violet walls of Jerusalem.

53. *Liberation*. 1937–52. Oil. France, Private Collection. The soldiers carrying flags, the musicians and the bright colors establish a joyous mood.

54. UPPER: *The Red Rooster*. 1952. Color lithograph. LOWER: *The Brown Horse*. 1952. Color lithograph.

55. *Good Morning over Paris*. 1952. Color lithograph.

56. *The Artist with a Palette and a Model*. 1952. Color lithograph. Detail of a poster made for an exhibition of prints in Nice.

57. *Visions of Paris*. 1952. Color lithograph.

58. *Banks on the Seine*. 1953. Oil. Owned by the artist's wife. One of more than thirty large paintings on Parisian themes. Do not miss the painter standing at his easel, beside the boats on the river bank.

59. *Red Roofs*. 1953. Oil. Owned by the artist. In the dark zone (upper left) the Seine River flows past Notre-Dame. In the center is "Vitebsk," with a Christ on the Cross in front of the domed church. The large red-robed figure is the painter. Note the man with a Torah scroll and, below, the strange creature consisting of the upper half of a boy and, reversed, the upper half of a bride.

60. *The Flute Player*. 1954. Gouache. France, Private Collection. This pastorale was painted by Chagall at Olympia, Greece, which he visited with his wife.

61. *Quai de Bercy*. 1952. Color lithograph.

62. *The Bastille*. 1954. Color lithograph. In the Place de la Bastille is the Colonne de Juillet, in honor of the heroes of the revolution of July, 1830.

63. UPPER LEFT: *Night in Paris*. 1952. Color lithograph. UPPER RIGHT:

Eiffel Tower with Donkey. 1954. Color lithograph. LOWER LEFT: *On Sundays.* 1954. Color lithograph. LOWER RIGHT: *Quai aux Fleurs.* 1954. Color lithograph.

64. *The White Window.* 1955. Oil. Owned by the artist. Through the many-paned window the landscape of Vence is softly indicated. Spring is in the air.

65. UPPER RIGHT: Black Water Pitcher. 1955. Pottery. LOWER LEFT: Red Dish. 1955. Pottery. In Vence, the artist began to make pottery—plates, vases and wall plaques—as well as sculptures. The motifs used are the same as in the paintings. Lines are often scratched in with the brush handle.

66. *The Bible.* 1956. A series of lithographs. UPPER LEFT: *King Solomon.* UPPER RIGHT: *King David and Bathsheba.* LOWER LEFT: *King David and Absalom.* LOWER RIGHT: *King David and His Harp.*

67. *Moses Breaking the Tablets of the Law.* 1955–56. Oil. Cologne, Wallraf-Richartz Museum. Moses has cast the tablets on the ground. At the right, people dance around the golden calf. At the left, on the edge of the mountain, a small group look mourningly at the destruction of the tablets. Above them is a very tall young man with a Torah in his arms. Next to him, a young couple stands under the bridal canopy.

68. *Equestrienne.* 1957. Color lithograph.

69. *Trick Cyclists.* 1957. Oil. Owned by the artist. This painting is composed of several sets of concentric circles.

70. UPPER: *The Red Rooster.* 1957. Color lithograph. LOWER: *The Accordion Player.* 1957. Color lithograph.

71. *The Lovers of Vence.* 1958. Oil. Germany, Private Collection.

72. *Clowns at Night.* 1957. Oil. Owned by the artist. This melancholy and haunting dark picture has none of the exuberant gaiety one associates with Chagall.

73. *Île Saint-Louis.* 1959. Color lithograph. The artist has a town residence in this old section of Paris.

74. *The Red Circus.* 1956–60. Oil. One of a series of pictures Chagall painted after seeing the filming of scenes for a movie at the Cirque d'Hiver, Paris.

75. *The Tree of Jesse.* 1960. Oil. Basel, Private Collection. The title refers to Christ's family ("And there shall come forth a rod out of the stem of Jesse, and a Branch shall grow out of his roots," Isaiah 11:1). Here a tree grows out of the church of Notre-Dame, Paris.

76. *Woman with Blue Face.* 1960. Oil. The general sombre effect suggests a night scene.

77. *The Bible.* 1958–59. Color lithographs. UPPER LEFT: *The Maid of Israel.* UPPER RIGHT: *The Garden of Eden.* LOWER LEFT: *The Garden of Eden.* LOWER RIGHT: *The Creation.*

78. *The Farmer.* 1961. Color lithograph.

79. *Daphnis and Chloë.* 1961. A series of color lithographs for a story from the world of ancient mythology. Commissioned by the Parisian publisher, Tériade, who, after Vollard's death, handled Chagall's graphic work. UPPER: *Springtime on the Meadow.* LOWER: *Phileta's Orchard.*

80. *Chloë Is Carried Off by the Methymneans.* (From the same series.)

81. UPPER LEFT: *Daphnis and Mycenion.* UPPER RIGHT: *The Summer Sea-*

son. LOWER LEFT: *The Dead Dolphin and the Three Hundred Drachmas.*
LOWER RIGHT: *Chloë.* (From the same series.)

82. UPPER: *Temple and History of Bacchus.* LOWER: *Megacles Recognizes his Daughter during the Feast.* (From the same series.)

83. *Moses and the Tablets of the Law.* 1962. Color lithograph. Poster for an exhibition, "Chagall and the Bible," held at Geneva.

84–91. *The Jerusalem Windows.* These twelve windows were commissioned by Hadassah, a Zionist women's organization, for the synagogue of its Hebrew University Medical Center near Jerusalem. They were executed in glass, from Chagall's designs, by Charles and Brigitte Simon Marq at Reims, France, in 1960 and 1961. Each window commemorates one of the twelve tribes.

84. *Levi.* Gouache.

85. *Levi.* Color lithograph (based on the window).

86. *Zebulun.* Gouache.

87. *Zebulun.* Color lithograph (based on the window).

88. *Joseph.* Color lithograph (based on the window).

89. *Joseph* (detail from Plate 88).

90. *Issachar.* Color lithograph (based on the window).

91. *Asher* (detail from the color lithograph, based on the window).

92. *Self-Portrait.* 1962. Oil. The seventy-five-year-old artist reconstructed the features of his youth, as well as scenes from a Vitebsk, long gone.

THE PLATES

1   Chagall in his studio at Vence.

2 UPPER: *The Little Parlor*. 1908. Oil. 8⅞ × 11⅜ in. France, Private Collection. LOWER: *Studio*. 1910. Oil. 23⅝ × 28¾ in. Owned by the artist.

3
Still Life with a Lamp. 1910.
Oil. 31⅞ × 17¾ in. Lucerne,
Private Collection. There is
here an affinity with the early
Kandinsky.

4 *Harvest*. 1910. Oil. 23⅝ × 31⅞ in. New York, Private Collection. Chagall apparently
agreed with the Fauves: that the artist must be nature's master, not her slave.

5 *Homage to Apollinaire*. 1911–12. Oil. 82⅞ × 78 in. Eindhoven, Stedelijk van Abbe-Museum. The central figure seems to proclaim the unity of man and woman.

6 *I and the Village*.   1911.   Oil.   75¼ × 59¼ in.   New York, The Museum of Modern Art.
This poetic picture, boldly defying logic and rationality, is one of Chagall's most famous works.

7 *The Holy Drosky Driver.* 1911. Oil. 58¼ × 46¼ in. Krefeld, Private Collection. The green body "drops like a meteor into the snowdrifts of Vitebsk" (Lionello Venturi).

8 *Self-Portrait with Seven Fingers.* 1912. Oil. 50⅜ × 42⅛ in. Amsterdam, Stedelijk Museum. The picture on the easel is entitled *To Russia, Asses and Others* (1911)

9 *The Poet, or Half-Past Three.*   1911.   Oil.   77⅝ × 57½ in.   Philadelphia, Museum of Art.
The poet's ecstasy is apparent in the upside-down head.

10 *Adam and Eve*. 1912. Oil. 63¼ × 42⅞ in. St. Louis, City Art Museum. This is perhaps the most Cubist picture Chagall ever produced.

11 *Still Life*. 1912. Oil. 24¾ × 30¾ in. London, Private Collection. While still lifes like
this were favorites of the Cubists, Chagall painted only a few.

12
Pregnant Woman. 1913.
Oil.   76⅜ × 45¼ in.   Amsterdam, Stedelijk Museum.
Chagall was influenced by Russian culture beyond the ghetto boundaries.

13 *The Soldier Drinks.* 1912–13. Oil. 43¼ × 37⅜ in. New York, The Solomon R. Guggenheim Museum. "The Russian folk song . . . has become an art song" (Walter Erben).

14 *Green Violinist.* 1918. Oil. 77¾ × 42¾ in. New York, The Solomon R. Guggenheim Museum. The fiddle was the favorite instrument of the Russian ghetto.

15 *Burning House*. 1913. Oil. 41⅞ × 47½ in. New York, The Solomon R. Guggenheim Museum. Here is Chagall, the color magician.

16 *Self-Portrait in Front of a House.* 1914. Oil. 19½ × 14⅞ in. Paris, Private Collection. Self-confident and elegantly dressed, Chagall stands before his parental home.

17 *Over Vitebsk.* 1914. Oil. 28¾ × 36½ in. Toronto, Private Collection. In Chagall's irrational world, men, as well as animals, can fly or float through the air.

18 *Lovers in Blue*. 1914. Oil. 19 × 17⅛ in. Leningrad, Private Collection. Jean Cassou writes that this picture is "completely bathed in celestial ultramarine."

19 *The Mirror*. 1915. Oil. 39⅜ × 31⅞ in. Leningrad, State Russian Museum. The yellow and green anticipate the abstractions of the 1960's.

20
Purim. 1916–18. Oil. 18⅞ × 27⅞ in. Philadelphia, Museum of Art. The title, Purim, is given in Hebrew characters (upper right corner).

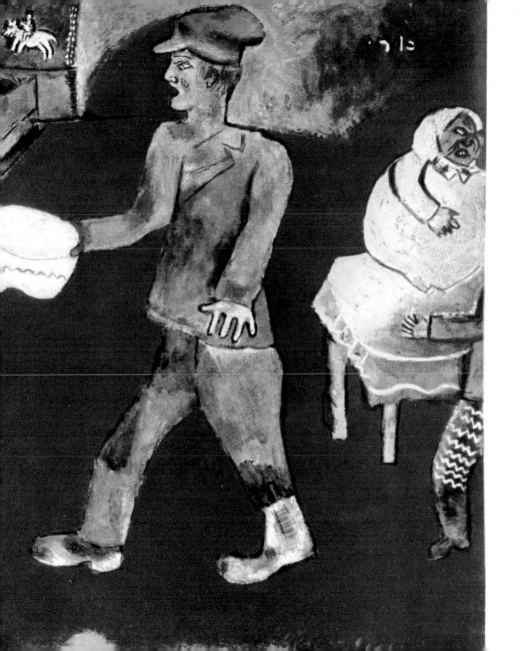

21
*Double Portrait
with Wineglass.*
1917. Oil. 91¾
× 53½ in. Paris,
Musée National
d'Art Moderne.
One of the major
works produced in
the year of the
Russian Revolu-
tion.

22 *Promenade*. 1917. Oil. 66⅞ × 64½ in. Leningrad, State Russian Museum. Note the Cubist clouds.

23 *Cemetery Gate*. 1917. Oil. 34¼ × 26⅞ in. Basel, Private Collection. The forms of the gate are echoed in the sky.

24 *The Lovers and the Lilies.* 1922–25. Oil. 44½ × 36 in. New York, Private Collection.
This tender picture heralds a new style.

25 *Double Portrait*. 1924. Oil. 51⅛ × 37 in. Paris, Private Collection. After nine years' marriage, Bella Chagall still appears as a bride.

26 *Ida at the Window*. 1924. Oil. 41⅜ × 29½ in. Amsterdam, Stedelijk Museum. Ida Chagall grew up to become a painter herself.

27 *Woman with Pigs*.   1926.   Gouache.   24½ × 18⅝ in.   Winnipeg, Private Collection.   Xeno-
phobic Frenchmen resented the choice of Chagall to illustrate a French classic.

28 *Equestrienne*. 1927. Oil. 39⅜ × 31⅞ in. Prague, Narodnie Galerie. The rider's dress looks like a flower still life.

29 *Flowers*. 1928. Oil. 46⅛ × 35 in. Paris, Private Collection. Note how freely and freshly brushed the flowers are!

30 *Bride and Groom with Eiffel Tower*. 1928. Oil. 35 × 45⅝ in. Paris, Private Collection.
Chagall lovingly called Paris "my second Vitebsk."

31 *The Girl Acrobat*. 1930. Oil. 25⅝ × 20½ in. Paris, Musée National d'Art Moderne. This could also be a scene from a ballet.

32 *Equestrienne.* 1931. Oil. 40 × 32½ in. Amsterdam, Stedelijk Museum. Why shouldn't a horse play a violin?

33
Bride and Bridegroom.
1930. Oil. $57 \times 35\frac{1}{2}$
in. Florida, Private
Collection. Chagall is
the painter of love *par
excellence.*

34 *The Wailing Wall.* 1932. Oil. 28⅜ × 36¼ in. Tel Aviv, Municipal Museum. The proportions of the wall are exaggerated by the tininess of the figures.

35 *The Lovers at the Eiffel Tower.* 1938–39. Oil. 55 × 54 in. This picture could have been called "The Wedding."

36 *Time Is a River without Banks.* 1939. Oil. 40½ × 32⅝ in. New York, The Museum of Modern Art. The lovers seem unaware of this strange apparition.

37 *The Cellist.* 1939. Oil. 39⅜ × 28¾ in. London, Private Collection. For this cellist, life and music seem to be identical.

38 *Obsession.* 1943. Oil. 30¼ × 42½ in. France, Private Collection. The figure of Christ on the Cross often appears in Chagall's middle period.

39 *War.* 1943. Oil. 41⅜ × 29⅞ in. Paris, Musée National d'Art Moderne. War as suffering, not as aggressive action.

40 *Listening to the Rooster*. 1944. Oil. 39 × 28⅛ in. New York, Private Collection. The strong red dominates this enigmatic picture.

41 *Around Her.* 1945. Oil. 51⅝ × 42⅞ in. Paris, Musée National d'Art Moderne. This "In Memoriam" was painted a few months after Bella Chagall's death.

42 *The Flying Sleigh.* 1945. Oil. 51⅛ × 27⅝ in. New York, Private Collection. After an absence of more than twenty years Chagall still recalled snow-covered Vitebsk.

43 *Autumn Village*. 1939–45. Oil. 32½ × 26 in. Hartford, Wadsworth Athenaeum. Fiddler, goat and bare-breasted woman seem comfortable on their odd perches.

44 *Self-Portrait with Wall Clock*. 1947. Oil. 33⅞ × 27⅞ in. Owned by the artist. No picture for those insisting that two plus two makes four!

45 *The Falling Angel.* 1923–47. Oil. 58¼ × 65⅜ in. Basel, Kunstmuseum. This combination of images produces a terrifying apocalyptic mood.

46 *The Dance* (detail). 1950. Oil. 91⅜ × 68⅞ in. Owned by the artist. Often in Chagall's work one color—here a melodious yellow—predominates.

47 *Arabian Nights.* 1941. Color lithograph. With his untrammeled fantasy, Chagall was just the man to illustrate Oriental tales.

Four
more
color
lithographs
from
*Arabian
Nights.*

49 *The Fishes at Saint-Jean.* 1949. Gouache. 31⅛ × 22⅞ in. Paris, Private Collection. The dreamy-faced lovers emerge from the deep-blue Mediterranean Sea.

50 *The Red Sun.* 1949. Oil. 55⅛ × 38⅝ in. Owned by the artist. The huge red disk is the sun.

51 *Blue Circus*.   1950.   Oil.   90½ × 68⅞ in.   Owned by the artist.   The moon is holding a fiddle.

52
King David. 1952.
76 × 31⅛ in.   Owned
by the artist.   This is
a capsule biography of
Israel's most beloved
king.

53
Liberation. **1937–52.** Oil. **67 ×
35 in.** France, Private Collection.
The artist appears twice, painting his
beloved and embracing her tenderly.

54   UPPER: *The Red Rooster*.   1952.   Color lithograph.   15 × 17¾ in.   LOWER: *The Brown Horse*.
1952.   Color litho.   15 × 17¾ in.   Chagall is one of this century's most prolific print makers.

55 *Good Morning over Paris.* 1952. Color lithograph. 18¾ × 21¾ in.

56 *The Artist with a Palette and a Model.* 1952. Color lithograph. 23½ × 19¾ in.

57 *Visions of Paris.* 1952. Color lithograph.

58 *Banks on the Seine*. 1953. Oil. 31⅛ × 26¾ in. Owned by the artist's wife. Chagall's style becomes freer and freer.

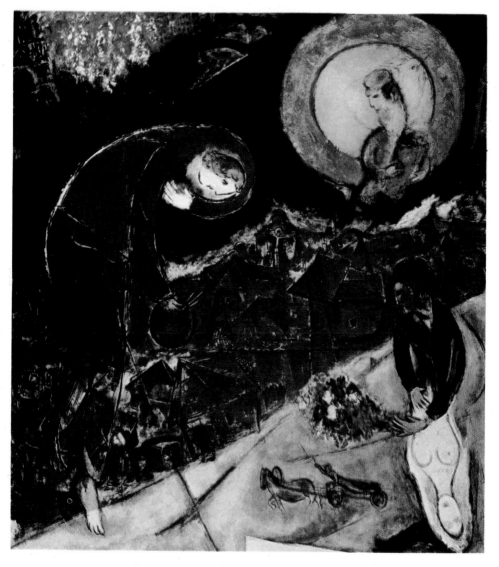

59 *Red Roofs.* 1953. Oil. 86⅝ × 83⅞ in. Owned by the artist. Remembrance of Vitebsk.

60 *The Flute Player*. 1954. Gouache. 24⅛ × 18⅞ in. France, Private Collection. As in Plate 27, the medium used is gouache, an opaque watercolor.

61
Quai de Bercy. 1952. Color lithograph.
26 × 38 in. Fantasy, color and superb
decorative sense induce an exquisite
mood of love and levitation.

62 *The Bastille*. 1954. Color lithograph. 20½ × 26¾ in. Chagall treats Paris poetically rather than topographically.

63 Color lithographs. UPPER LEFT: *Night in Paris*. 1952. 13½ × 11 in. UPPER RIGHT: *Eiffel Tower with Donkey*. 1954. 15½ × 11 in. LOWER LEFT: *On Sundays*. 1954. 15¾ × 11 in. LOWER RIGHT: *Quai aux Fleurs*. 1954. 14 × 10¼ in.

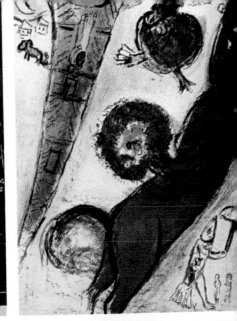

64 *The White Window*. 1955. Oil. 58 × 47 in. Owned by the artist. The pigments are only thinly applied (see also Plate 26).

65 UPPER RIGHT: Black Water Pitcher.   Pottery.   1955.   LOWER LEFT: Red Dish.   Pottery.
1955.   Chagall studied in pottery workshops at Antibes, Vence and Vallauris.

66
The Bible.
1956. Color
lithographs.
King Solomon.
David and
Bathsheba.
King David
and Absalom.
King David
and His Harp.

67 *Moses Breaking the Tablets of the Law.* 1955–56. Oil. 89¾ × 59⅞ in. Cologne, Wallraf-Richartz Museum. This picture was preceded by *Moses Receiving the Tablets of the Law* (1950–52).

68 *Equestrienne.* 1957. Color lithograph. 13 × 10 in. Chagall's animals are not to be found in zoology textbooks.

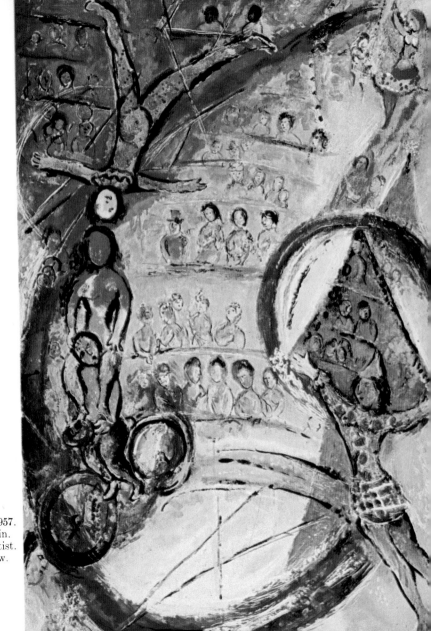

69
Trick Cyclists. 1957.
Oil. 59⅞ × 39⅜ in.
Owned by the artist.
A veritable rainbow.

70 Color lithographs.   UPPER: *The Red Rooster*.   1957.   10 × 15 in.   LOWER: *The Accordion Player*.   1957.   10 × 16 in.

71 *The Lovers of Vence.* 1958. Oil. 24¼ × 39¾ in. Germany, Private Collection. Like many ancient towns of southern France, Vence is built on a hill.

72 *Clowns at Night.* 1957. Oil. 37⅜ × 37⅜ in. Owned by the artist. There is a resigned sadness on the face of the fiddler.

73 *Île Saint-Louis.* 1959. Color lithograph. 20¼ × 26½ in.

74 *The Red Circus.* 1956–60. Oil. A symphony in red.

75 *The Tree of Jesse*.   1960.   Oil.   59 × 47¼ in.   Basel, Private Collection.   Chagall is at the easel, painting a picture of Paris.

76 *Woman with Blue Face.* 1960. Oil. 39⅞ × 31⅞ in. Chagall's recent pictures are anthologies.

77
The
Bible.
1958–59.
Color
litho-
graphs.

78 *The Farmer*. 1961. Color lithograph. 12 × 9½ in.

79 *Daphnis and Chloë.* 1961. Color lithographs. UPPER: *Springtime on the Meadow.* LOWER: *Phileta's Orchard.* Each 13½ × 16¼ in. This ancient myth of two abandoned children.

80 *Chloë is Carried off by the Methymneans* (from the same series). 13½ × 16¼ in.

81
*Daphnis
and Chloë*.
1961.
Color
lithographs.
Each 16¼ ×
12¾ in.

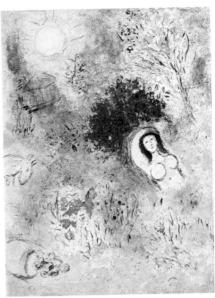

82 UPPER: *Temple and History of Bacchus*. LOWER: *Megacles Recognizes his Daughter during the Feast*. 12¾ × 16¼ in. (From the same series.)

83 *Moses and the Tablets of the Law.* 1962. Color lithograph.

84 *The Jerusalem Windows.* 1960–61. Each of the windows *ca.* 11 feet high and 8 feet wide. *Levi.* Gouache.

85. *Levi.* Color lithograph. 33 × 25½ in.

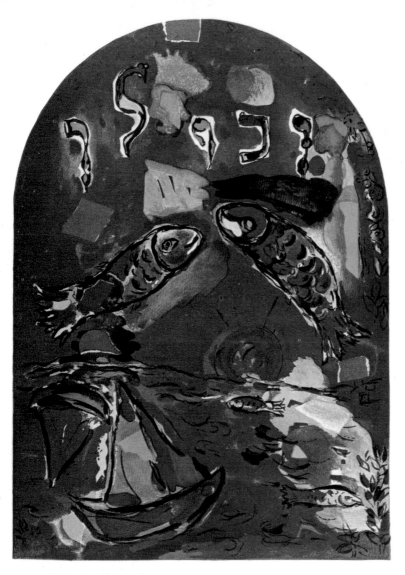

86 *Zebulun*. Gouache.

87 *Zebulun.* Color lithograph. 33 × 25½ in.

88 *Joseph.* Color lithograph. 33 × 25½ in.

89 *Joseph* (detail from Plate 88).

ישׂשׂכר
חמר גרם
רבץ מבין
המשׁפתים

90 *Issachar.*   Color lithograph.   33 × 25½ in.

90 *Issachar.* Color lithograph. 33 × 25½ in.

89 *Joseph* (detail from Plate 88).

92 *Self-Portrait*. 1962. Oil. 27 × 20 in. A loving, protecting woman is never far from Chagall.

91 *Asher* (detail from the color lithograph)